The Symphony of Words

Orchestrating Change with NLP

Rex Morton

Copyright Page

© 2023 by Rex Morton

All rights reserved. No part of this book may be reproduced in any form or by any electronic or mechanical means, including information storage and retrieval systems, without permission in writing from the publisher, except by a reviewer who may quote brief passages in a review.

This book is a work of non-fiction. Unless otherwise noted, the author and the publisher make no explicit guarantees about the accuracy of the information in this book and will not be held responsible for any errors or omissions.

Published by Omniterra Media Inc

First Edition

Visit the author's website at www.rexmorton.com

For information regarding special discounts for bulk purchases, please contact Rex Morton Publishing Special Sales at rex@rexmorton.com.

Disclaimer

This book is intended to provide information about the fields of Neuro-Linguistic Programming (NLP) and Cognitive Behavioural Therapy (CBT) and their potential integration. While the author has made every effort to ensure that the information was correct at the time of publication, the author does not assume and hereby disclaims any liability to any party for any loss, damage, or disruption caused by errors or omissions, whether such errors or omissions result from negligence, accident, or any other cause.

The contents of this book should not be used as a substitute for professional advice, diagnosis, or treatment. The reader should always consult a qualified healthcare provider about mental health concerns or conditions. Never disregard professional psychological or medical advice or delay in seeking it because of something you have read in this book.

The views expressed in this work are solely those of the author and do not necessarily reflect the views of the publisher, and the publisher hereby disclaims any responsibility for them.

Including websites, links, or references to other resources does not mean that the author or the publisher endorses the information the organization or website may provide or its recommendations. Furthermore, the author does not guarantee the accuracy of these resources' information.

The use of any information provided in this book is solely at your own risk.

Chapter 1: Introduction - The Symphony of Transformation

Welcome to a New World of Harmony

Imagine stepping into a world where words create music, a world where the rhythm of language shapes our lives, much like a composer shapes a symphony. This is the world of Neuro-Linguistic Programming (NLP), a fascinating realm where the power of language and thought converge to create a profound impact on our personal and professional lives. In this chapter, we'll embark on a journey to understand NLP and explore the unique perspective of this book: comparing NLP to the art of composing music.

What is NLP?

Neuro-Linguistic Programming, or NLP for short, might sound like a complex term, but it's actually based on a simple yet powerful idea. It's about how we use our language (Linguistic) and thoughts (Neuro) to program (Programming) the way we experience the world and how we respond to it. Think of NLP as a toolkit for the mind, packed with techniques and insights that help us understand and influence our thoughts, feelings, and behaviors.

NLP in Everyday Life

Have you ever wondered why certain words can lift your spirits while others can bring you down? Or why some people seem to have a magic touch when it comes to communication and persuasion? NLP provides answers to these questions. It teaches us how to use language to positively influence our thoughts and emotions, and how to communicate more effectively with others. Whether it's improving relationships, excelling in your career, or simply gaining more confidence, NLP offers a path to achieving these goals.

The Music of NLP

But what does NLP have to do with music? Just as a composer uses different notes, rhythms, and harmonies to create an emotional impact through music, NLP uses the elements of language and thought to create positive changes in our lives. In this book, we'll explore this analogy in depth, showing you how to become the composer of your own life's symphony.

The Rhythm of Change

Just like a symphony, our lives are full of different movements - highs and lows, fast-paced moments, and times of quiet reflection. NLP teaches us how to navigate these movements gracefully, using the power of language and thought to maintain harmony and balance. By the end of this book, you'll learn how to use NLP techniques to compose a life that resonates with your deepest desires and values.

Embarking on a Harmonious Journey

As we begin this journey together, remember that NLP is not just a set of theories; it's a practical approach to life. Each chapter of this book will provide you with insights and exercises that you can apply immediately, helping you to orchestrate positive changes in your life. So, get ready to tune your mind to the beautiful symphony of words, and let's embark on this transformative journey together.

Chapter 2: The Foundations of NLP and Music - Understanding the Basics

A Symphony of Thoughts and Sounds

Welcome to the chapter where we blend the worlds of Neuro-Linguistic Programming (NLP) and music. Here, we'll uncover the basic building blocks of both NLP and music - understanding how they work separately and how, surprisingly, they share many similarities. Think of it as learning the notes before playing a melody.

The Building Blocks of NLP

NLP has three main components, much like the essentials in a musician's toolkit. Let's explore these in a simple, easy-to-understand way:

Representational Systems: This is about how we experience the world through our senses. Just like we use our eyes to see and ears to hear, our mind uses these systems to understand the world. Some of us might be more visual (seeing), others more auditory (hearing), or kinesthetic (feeling). Knowing this helps us understand how we and others think and feel.

Meta-Model: This part of NLP is like a detective's tool. It helps us ask questions to uncover the deeper meaning behind the words people use. It's about clarifying, understanding, and getting to the heart of communication.

Milton Model: Named after Milton Erickson, a famous therapist, this model is all about using language in a way that's vague and metaphorical. It's like telling a story that lets people find their own meaning and solutions.

The Essentials of Music

Music, on the other hand, is built on three key elements:

Rhythm: This is the beat - the tapping of your foot, the clapping of your hands. It's the timing and pace of the music.

Melody: This is the tune that you hum or sing. It's the series of notes that catch your ear and often stick in your mind.

Harmony: This is about notes being played together to create depth and emotion. It's what makes music rich and fulfilling.

Finding Harmony Between NLP and Music

Now, let's draw parallels between these elements. In a way, representational systems in NLP are like the rhythm in music. They set the pace and tone of our thoughts and communication. The Meta-Model, like a melody, helps us navigate through the surface to find the underlying tune of what someone is really saying. And the

Milton Model? It's the harmony - creating a depth of meaning and allowing for personal interpretation.

Understanding these basics of NLP and music sets the stage for a deeper exploration. It's like learning the scales before playing a full piece. As we move forward, we'll see how these elements work together to create a symphony of effective communication and personal growth, much like how rhythm, melody, and harmony come together to create beautiful music.

So, stay tuned, and let's dive deeper into this fascinating journey where words meet melodies, and thoughts dance to the rhythm of change.

Chapter 3: Language as Rhythm - The Beat of Communication

The Music of Words

Welcome to a chapter where we explore the rhythm in language - how it influences our thoughts, emotions, and ultimately, our actions. Just as the rhythm in music moves us, the rhythm of our language shapes our experiences. Let's delve into this intriguing aspect of communication, drawing parallels with the rhythmic pulse of music.

The Rhythm of Language

Have you ever noticed how the pace of your speech quickens when you're excited or slows down when you're sad? This is the rhythm of language at play. It's not just about what we say, but how we say it - the tempo, the pauses, the emphasis. These patterns in our speech impact not only how we feel but also how others perceive and respond to us.

The Power of Rhythmic Words

Just like a catchy drumbeat can energize us, rhythmic patterns in language can influence our thinking and behavior. A well-timed pause can create suspense, a rapid succession of words can convey urgency, and a slow, measured pace can soothe and calm. This rhythm in our speech can amplify our message, making it more powerful and impactful.

Music and Emotions: A Parallel

In music, rhythm sets the mood. A fast-paced beat gets your heart racing, ready for action, while a slow, steady rhythm can be calming and relaxing. Similarly, the rhythm of our language can affect our emotions and those of our listeners. It's a tool we can use to convey excitement, urgency, calmness, or any other emotion we wish to express.

Exercises to Develop Rhythmic Communication Skills

Pace Variation: Practice changing the speed of your speech. Try reading a paragraph slowly, then quickly. Notice how the different paces change the feel of the words.

Pause for Effect: When speaking, use pauses to emphasize a point. You can practice this by reading aloud and intentionally pausing at key moments.

Emphasis on Key Words: Like a drummer accentuates certain beats, try emphasizing key words in your sentences. This can change the 'beat' of your message and make it more memorable.

Rhythm Replication: Listen to a piece of music and try to match your speech rhythm to the beat of the music. This can be a fun way to experiment with different rhythmic patterns in language.

Emotional Speech: Try expressing different emotions through your speech. Speak angrily, happily, sadly, and notice how your rhythm changes with each emotion.

The Symphony of Conversation

As we become more aware of the rhythm in our language, we can start to use it deliberately, like a musician uses rhythm to create a certain mood or feeling in their music. This awareness and control over our speech's rhythm can transform our communication, making it more effective and expressive.

So, let's embrace the rhythm in our words, using it to enhance our communication and connect more deeply with those around us. Like a beautiful piece of music, our conversations can become more engaging, impactful, and harmonious.

Chapter 4: Harmonizing Thoughts with Words - Crafting the Melody of the Mind

Finding Harmony in Communication

In this chapter, we step into the world of harmony – not just in music, but in our thoughts and words. Just as a harmonious melody can soothe the soul, harmonious language can bring peace and positivity to our minds. Let's explore how the words we choose shape our thoughts, and how we can use language to create a harmonious inner world.

The Impact of Words on Thoughts

Words are powerful. They have the ability to uplift us or bring us down, to create conflict or foster understanding. Think of your thoughts as a stream of words running through your mind. When these words are negative or jarring, they can create discord, much like an off-key note in a song. Conversely, positive, affirming words can create harmony, soothing and aligning our thoughts with our goals and desires.

Creating Harmonic Sequences in Language

In music, harmony is achieved when notes are combined in a way that is pleasing to the ear. Similarly, in language, harmony is achieved when words are combined in a way that creates a positive, coherent message. Here are some techniques to align your language with your desired outcomes:

Positive Framing: Shift your language from negative to positive. Instead of saying, "I can't handle this," try, "I'm finding new ways to cope."

Affirmations: Use positive statements about yourself and your abilities. Repeat affirmations like, "I am capable and strong," to build a harmonious mindset.

Empathetic Language: When communicating with others, use words that show understanding and empathy. Phrases like, "I see what you mean," or, "I understand how you feel," can create a sense of harmony in conversations.

Question for Clarity: Ask questions to understand others better, rather than making assumptions. This helps in creating a harmonious dialogue.

Hypothetical Case Studies: The Power of Harmonious Language

Let's look at hypothetical examples to see the power of harmonious language in action:

Hypothetical Case Study 1: A manager who used harsh, critical language noticed high turnover in his team. After shifting to a more positive and supportive language, the morale and retention rate improved dramatically.

Hypothetical Case Study 2: A person struggling with self-confidence began using daily affirmations. Over time, this practice led to a significant increase in their self-esteem and overall well-being.

Hypothetical Case Study 3: In a relationship filled with misunderstandings, a couple started using empathetic language to express their feelings. This change brought about a deeper understanding and strengthened their bond.

Crafting Your Inner Symphony

As we learn to use language that aligns with our desired outcomes, we begin to create a harmonious inner world. Our thoughts become more positive, our interactions become more meaningful, and our lives start to reflect the harmony we've created with our words.

In this chapter, we've seen how powerful language can be in shaping our thoughts and experiences. As we move forward, let's keep in mind that every word we choose is a note in the melody of our lives. By choosing our words wisely, we can compose a beautiful, harmonious symphony of thoughts and experiences.

Chapter 5: Composing Life's Symphony with NLP - Creating Your Masterpiece

Orchestrating Change

In this chapter, we delve into the art of using NLP (Neuro-Linguistic Programming) techniques to compose the symphony of our lives, just as a composer uses musical elements to create a breathtaking piece of music. We'll explore how NLP can be a powerful tool in orchestrating personal and professional growth, and share inspiring stories of transformation.

NLP: The Composer's Toolkit

Think of NLP as a composer's toolkit, filled with various instruments and notes (techniques and strategies) that can be used to create a harmonious life symphony. Just as a composer carefully selects each note and instrument to create a desired mood or theme, you can use NLP techniques to shape your thoughts, feelings, and actions to align with your goals.

Strategies for Harmonious Living

Setting the Tone: Like choosing the key in music, set the tone of your life by defining clear, positive goals. Use NLP's goal-setting techniques to clarify what you truly want to achieve.

Creating Rhythms of Success: Develop daily habits and routines that support your goals. Just as a steady rhythm is crucial in music, consistent actions create the rhythm of success in life.

Balancing the Melody and Harmony: Balance your personal and professional life, like a composer balances melody and harmony. Use NLP techniques to manage your emotions and relationships, ensuring each aspect of your life complements the others.

Crafting Your Unique Composition: Remember, your life's symphony is unique. Use NLP to embrace and enhance your personal strengths, much like a composer uses their signature style.

Hypothetical Stories of Transformation

The Overwhelmed Executive: John, a high-level executive, felt overwhelmed by stress and poor work-life balance. Through NLP, he learned to reframe his thoughts, set achievable goals, and manage his time effectively. Like a fine-tuned composition, he transformed his life into a harmonious balance of work and personal fulfillment.

The Aspiring Artist: Emma, an artist plagued with self-doubt, used NLP techniques to build confidence and visualize success. She began to see her career as a canvas for her creativity, leading to a series of successful exhibitions.

The Rejuvenated Teacher: Mark, a teacher losing passion for his job, utilized NLP to rediscover his love for teaching. By changing his internal dialogue, he reignited his enthusiasm and positively impacted his students.

Your Life, Your Symphony

As we conclude this chapter, remember that you are the composer of your life. With NLP as your toolkit, you have the power to create a masterpiece of your existence. Each technique you apply, every positive change you make, is a note in the beautiful symphony that is your life. Embrace the process of composing, and watch as your life transforms into a harmonious, fulfilling masterpiece.

Chapter 6: NLP Techniques as Musical Scales - Tuning Your Skills for Harmony

Practicing the Scales of Self-Improvement

Welcome to a chapter where we connect the discipline of practicing musical scales to mastering NLP techniques. Just as a musician diligently practices scales to improve their music, we can use NLP exercises regularly to enhance our communication skills and personal development. Let's explore some practical exercises and see how incorporating them into our daily routine can create a symphony of positive change in our lives.

NLP Exercises: Your Daily Scales

Visualizing Success: Just like playing a scale helps a musician visualize a melody, this exercise helps you picture your goals. Each morning, spend a few minutes visualizing your ideal day or a specific goal as vividly as possible. See it, feel it, hear it.

Positive Affirmations: Like a scale that sets the tone for a piece, affirmations set the tone for your day. Create a list of positive statements about yourself and your abilities. Repeat them daily, feeling the truth in each word.

Active Listening Drill: Improving listening skills is like perfecting a musical rhythm. Practice paying close attention to the other person during conversations, acknowledging what they say, and giving intelligent answers. This enhances understanding and rapport.

Reframing Challenges: This exercise is about turning a dissonant note into a harmonious one. When faced with a challenge, take a moment to reframe it positively. Ask yourself, "What can I learn from this?" or "How can this make me stronger?"

Empathy Practice: Harmonizing with others' emotions is key in both music and life. Try to understand others' perspectives and feelings without judgment. This deepens connections and improves communication.

Building a Routine of NLP Practice

Incorporating these exercises into your daily life can be as simple as a musician practicing scales:

Morning Routine: Start your day with visualization and affirmations. This sets a positive tone for the day.

Throughout the Day: Use active listening in your conversations. This keeps your communication skills sharp.

Evening Reflection: End your day by reflecting on any challenges. Practice reframing them positively, just like resolving a dissonant chord in music.

The Harmony of Consistent Practice

Remember, the beauty of music doesn't come from playing scales once; it's the result of consistent practice. Similarly, the true benefits of these NLP exercises are seen when they become a regular part of your life. Your perspective, communication abilities, and general well-being will all gradually but significantly improve as you keep using these strategies.

Your Ongoing Symphony

As we conclude this chapter, think of your life as an ongoing symphony. Each day, with each NLP exercise, you are adding notes, rhythms, and harmonies to this symphony. The regular practice of these exercises isn't just a routine; it's the composition of a more harmonious, fulfilling life. Keep practicing your scales of NLP, and watch as the music of your life becomes richer and more beautiful.

Chapter 7: The Conductor's Baton - Leading with NLP

Orchestrating Leadership

Imagine a conductor leading an orchestra, each movement of the baton bringing forth a beautiful harmony of sounds. Similarly, in the world of leadership, the right techniques can create a symphony of effective teamwork and positive influence. In this chapter, we explore how the principles of NLP (Neuro-Linguistic Programming) can be used to enhance leadership skills, akin to a conductor directing a magnificent musical performance.

Leadership Through the Lens of NLP

Leadership, much like music conducting, is about creating harmony in a group, guiding and inspiring people to work together towards a common goal. NLP provides tools for understanding and influencing others effectively, enhancing communication, and fostering a positive environment.

Hypothetical Case Studies: Leaders Who Mastered the NLP Symphony

The Transformative CEO: Sarah, a CEO of a struggling company, used NLP techniques to understand her employees' perspectives and motivate them. By actively listening and empathizing, she fostered a culture of open communication and innovation, leading to a remarkable turnaround in company performance.

The Inspirational Educator: Mark, a high school principal, utilized NLP to build rapport with both teachers and students. He practiced positive language and reframing techniques to address challenges, which led to a significant improvement in school morale and student performance.

The Community Leader: Anita, who led a community project, used NLP to bring diverse groups together. By using empathetic and inclusive language, she was able to create a sense of unity and collaboration, achieving remarkable results in community development.

Tips for Becoming a Conductor of Your Life

Understand Your Orchestra: Just as a conductor must understand each musician, a leader should understand the people they are leading. Use NLP techniques to listen actively and empathize with others' viewpoints.

Set the Tempo: Determine the pace and direction for your team. Use clear, positive communication to set goals and expectations, much like a conductor sets the tempo for a piece.

Harmonize Your Team: Encourage teamwork and collaboration. Acknowledge individual strengths and show how they contribute to the team's overall success.

Adapt Your Style: Just as a conductor adjusts to different musical pieces, be flexible in your leadership style. Adapt to different situations and individual needs.

Lead with Confidence: Believe in your ability to lead and inspire. Confidence, like a conductor's decisive movements, can motivate and energize your team.

Conducting Your Symphony

In leadership, as in music, the harmony and success of the performance depend largely on the skill of the conductor. By applying NLP techniques in your leadership style, you can effectively guide and inspire others, creating a symphony of teamwork, progress, and positive influence. Remember, every great conductor started with learning the basics. As you practice these NLP strategies, you'll grow into the conductor of your life's symphony, leading with skill, grace, and confidence.

Chapter 8: Overcoming Life's Dissonances - Resolving Challenges with NLP

Tuning into Harmony

In music, dissonance is a clash of notes that creates tension, needing resolution to return to harmony. Similarly, in life, we face challenges and conflicts that can disrupt our inner peace. This chapter focuses on using NLP (Neuro-Linguistic Programming) techniques to address and overcome these dissonances, restoring harmony to our lives.

Addressing Challenges with NLP

NLP offers a set of tools and techniques to help us understand and manage our reactions to life's challenges. Like a composer resolving a musical dissonance, we can use NLP to transform our conflicts and obstacles into opportunities for growth and learning.

Coping Strategies for Harmony

Reframing Perspectives: One powerful NLP technique is reframing, which involves changing how we view a situation. For example, instead of seeing a mistake as a failure, reframe it as a learning opportunity. This shift in perspective can turn a negative experience into a positive one.

Changing the Narrative: Our internal dialogue greatly influences how we feel and act. By consciously changing our self-talk to be more positive and supportive, we can reduce the emotional impact of challenges.

Visualizing Solutions: Visualization is a common practice in both NLP and music composition. Imagine the best possible outcome in a challenging situation. This visualization can guide your actions and thoughts toward making that outcome a reality.

Empathetic Communication: Just as harmony in music requires different notes to work together, resolving conflicts often involves understanding and collaborating with others. Use empathetic listening and communication to find common ground and solutions.

Hypothetical Examples of Overcoming Obstacles

The Stressed Manager: Emily, a project manager, was overwhelmed by workplace stress. Through NLP, she learned to reframe her challenges and visualize successful project outcomes. This not only reduced her stress but also improved her team's performance.

The Fearful Public Speaker: Alex had a fear of public speaking. By using NLP techniques like positive self-talk and visualization, he overcame his fear and became a confident speaker, capable of engaging his audience effectively.

The Family Conflict: Sarah and her sister had a longstanding conflict. Through empathetic communication and understanding each other's perspectives, they resolved their differences and strengthened their relationship.

Finding Harmony in Dissonance

Just as a skilled composer uses dissonance to enhance the beauty of a musical piece, we can use life's challenges to grow and strengthen ourselves. By applying NLP techniques to our daily lives, we can transform conflicts and obstacles into harmonious resolutions. Remember, every dissonance in life is an opportunity to create a more beautiful and meaningful symphony.

Chapter 9: The Finale - Integrating NLP into Everyday Life

Encore: Making NLP a Part of Your Daily Symphony

As we reach the finale of our journey through the world of NLP (Neuro-Linguistic Programming) and its parallels with music, let's take a moment to reflect on the key takeaways from this book and how you can continue to incorporate these lessons into your daily life, turning your everyday experiences into a symphony of personal growth and transformation.

Key Takeaways from Our NLP Symphony

Language as Rhythm: Just as rhythm is essential in music, the rhythm of our language shapes our thoughts and interactions. Remember the power of pacing, tone, and emphasis in your communication.

Harmonizing Thoughts and Words: Like creating harmony in music, aligning your thoughts and words positively can create harmony in your life. Use affirmations and positive self-talk to maintain this harmony.

Composing Life with NLP: You have the power to be the composer of your life's symphony. Use NLP techniques to set goals, visualize success, and create the life you desire.

Practicing NLP Scales: Regular practice of NLP techniques, like practicing musical scales, is essential for mastery. Incorporate simple exercises like visualization and positive framing into your daily routine.

Leading with the Conductor's Baton: In leadership, as in conducting, it's about bringing out the best in others. Use empathy, clear communication, and understanding to lead effectively.

Resolving Life's Dissonances: Face challenges and conflicts with the mindset of resolving dissonance in music. Reframe challenges, change your internal narrative, and visualize positive outcomes.

Continuing Your NLP Practice

Like any skill, the benefits of NLP are most pronounced with consistent practice. Here are some tips to integrate NLP into your daily life:

Start Small: Choose one or two NLP techniques to focus on initially. Practice them until they become a natural part of your routine.

Reflect Daily: Spend a few minutes each day reflecting on your use of NLP. What worked well? What could be improved?

Stay Curious and Open: Be open to learning and experimenting with different NLP strategies. Each day offers new opportunities to apply these techniques.

Final Thoughts on Your Transformational Journey

As we conclude this book, think of the journey of personal transformation through the symphony of words as an ongoing composition. Each day brings new notes, rhythms, and harmonies to your life's music. The practice and application of NLP are not just for today but for a lifetime of growth, learning, and harmony.

Remember, the beauty of a symphony lies not just in its individual notes but in how they come together to create something greater. Similarly, the beauty of your life's symphony will unfold as you integrate the lessons of NLP into your everyday experiences, creating a masterpiece of personal fulfillment and achievement.

Thank you for joining me on this harmonious journey. May the symphony of your life be rich, beautiful, and endlessly evolving.

About the Author

Rex Morton is a renowned author and researcher in the United Kingdom with a passionate interest in the human mind, specifically in Cognitive Behavioural Therapy (CBT) and Neuro-Linguistic Programming (NLP).

Morton has spent a considerable portion of his professional life diving deep into the theories and principles that form the backbone of these two compelling fields.

Although Morton does not have clinical experience, his intense curiosity and dedication to studying these subjects have made him a respected figure in the field. He has thoroughly researched the integration of NLP techniques into CBT, offering fresh perspectives and insights into how these two methodologies can complement each other to enhance understanding of human cognition and Behaviour.

As an author, Morton has successfully communicated his knowledge and passion to a broader audience, making complex psychological theories accessible to professionals and interested laypersons. His writing is characterized by a clear, engaging style and a focus on the practical application of theories, making them relevant to everyday life.

In his personal life, Morton is an ardent lover of the natural world, often spending his free time exploring the British countryside. His passion for landscape photography allows him to capture and share the beauty of these excursions. Despite his accomplishments, Morton is known for his humility and eagerness to continue learning. His work continues to inspire those interested in the intricate workings of the human mind and the exciting possibilities presented by the integration of NLP and CBT.

Join the Journey at
RexMorton.com

If you've found the content of this book enlightening and wish to continue your journey of understanding the human mind, I warmly invite you to visit my website at www.rexmorton.com. The website serves as a hub of knowledge where I share my latest findings, thoughts, and insights on NLP and related topics.

I also encourage you to subscribe to the newsletter available on the website. By subscribing, you'll receive regular updates on a range of topics, from detailed discussions on specific NLP techniques and their application in other fields to the latest research.

The newsletter is also the first place I'll share news of upcoming releases. Whether it's the announcement of a new book, the launch of an online course, newsletter subscribers will be the first to know. This is a great opportunity to continue learning directly from me, deepening your understanding of NLP and related topics, and enhancing your skills in applying these techniques in your own life or professional practice.

I'm looking forward to sharing this journey with you.

www.ingramcontent.com/pod-product-compliance
Lightning Source LLC
Chambersburg PA
CBHW060905260726
48661CB00008B/3467